DESPAIR TO REPAIR

DESPAIR TO REPAIR

A POETRY COLLECTION OF
ADDICTION, RECOVERY, AND LIFE

CORY BEASLEY

WALNUT STREET
—PUBLISHING—

ISBN: 9798987389263

Walnut Street Publishing
5113 SR-58 A6
Chattanooga, TN 37416
www.walnutstreetpublishing.com

DEDICATION

I'd like to dedicate this collection to anyone who may be struggling, hurting, or lost. There is help and hope.

To my daughter. May you always fight to find the light.

To Sharie. Thank you for encouraging me to pursue my writing and being there during my struggles.

And to my past self. I wouldn't be the man I am today without you holding on for so long.

A LETTER TO MYSELF

Dear Cory,

I love you dude. The attributes I've allowed to be snuffed out due to trauma and life, I yearn for. Your kindness, the radiant gentleness, the never-ending desire to offer a hand to lift those that are down, and the beautiful ways you experience joy from even the smallest of things. I wasn't able to keep you in full, though I can say I'm steadily pulling from the darkness now. I've learned and have grown a lot. I am so proud of you for doing the best you could and feel relief knowing that you are starting to resurface. I refuse to do this alone and with you, we will never have to. We can do this.

Love,
Cory

Glimpse

What do others see?
A question
that would solve
problem after problem.
What would you see
when I dance
alone and unhindered,
when I sing
loudly,
at a one-man rendition
of pure emotion,
when I give
my lunch, my change,
my fabrication of worth
to help
those bound by struggle,
when I rage at strangers
for adding mere seconds
to my lengthy day,
when I slow down
to allow the passage,
as if seconds
mean nothing,
when I've belittled
and abused,
those I claim to love.
What would you see when
I giggle at my mind,
being silly and odd,
when I laugh
heartily
at my own joke that no one else
would have enjoyed,
when I turn red

from enjoyment
at inappropriate moments,
when I forget
that I'm an adult
at the sight
of a red panda,
or you.
What would you see,
if you only had
a glimpse
of the unfiltered
raw moments,
that live within my story,
and the chapters
of a few others
books?

Exhibit

Observing,
beautiful creations
bestowed to us,
by God
or Mother,
whichever
is easier to digest.
Though entranced,
my soul
cries.
My mind wanders,
from awe to hate.
Man,
claiming all,
enslaving all,
even me
even you.
Are we
any more free
than this
artificial habitat?
Though my thoughts
 teeter between
rage and admiration,
they focus intently,
on the one
exhibit that demands
my attention,
yielding
quite the smirk.
You.

Dream

Watch me grow.
Watch me dream.
Watch me tear apart
at the seam.
Digging deep
to find the source,
kicking and screaming
until I'm hoarse.
Treading within the dark
until it gleams,
illuminating the piece of me
from my dreams.
Replacing it all,
this worn thin stuffing,
with love and care
for my new becoming.
Pulling myself up
without a hitch,
carefully mending
with sow and stitch.
Admiring the effort
in my revival,
no longer living
for pure survival.
Chasing a dream
of whom I should be,
realizing sweetly
I am already me.

Blessed

Blessed in ways
that escape my belief,
comforting and carrying only relief.
Spiritually cleansing more decay,
living my life just for today.
Answering my prayers for a better day,
my doubts and fears he did sway.
Releasing the past was such a gift,
call it the present a change and shift.
Dreading the future was such a trip,
awaiting another unfortunate slip.
No longer bound to such a fate,
I won't be standing before death's gate.
The path is true and steady,
finally I don't doubt I'm ready.
My love is here within my heart,
my way of hate I did depart.
Finding the way to no longer obsess,
my will and my life he did bless.

Home

Time flows differently here.
You'll find no clocks,
just the pace of our minds, our breaths.
No lighting, natural illumination
bouncing from our eyes within every
shared moment.
Heated by proximity, chilled by goosebumps.
Both achieved by way of touch.
Appetite satisfied by the taste of us.
Music echoing, the lyrics
our conversation, our laughter
to the beat of our hearts.
Sheltered by the canopy of our souls.

Zero

Marvelous, this advancement.
Lights dance in our hands,
captivating mind and heart.
One hundred percent.
Wondrous, this era.
Connection sparks across a world,
uniting the unheard masses. Seventy percent.
Entertaining this technology.
Joyous moments shared instantly, uplifting
friends and family.
Fifty percent.
Instant, this gratification.
Frantically search, to replenish,
as your mood falters.
What could be wrong? Forty percent.
Laughter at dogs and cats as Max
and Mittens cry to play beside you.
What could be wrong? Thirty percent.
Awe and wonder, at the giggles of infants,
as your own is poisoned by your very fate.
What could be wrong?
Twenty percent. Hurry up now.
Drive faster, risk more risk others,
as you race to replace the time
you've misplaced. Ten percent...
Is all that is left.
There is no port or block, no outlet in sight.
How, will you laugh? How, will you smile?
Now, you can't connect. Five percent... is all
that is left. Anxiety fills thoughts race panic ensues.
You can't recharge nor replace,
for the battery was your life,
you've wasted away. Zero per...

Pot

You found my seed
within the forest.
Oblivious
of what I am,
you confined me to your pot.
You placed me
in the window,
teasing me, with the sun.
You watered my soil,
but never me.
Still, I bloomed
a beautiful flower
for you
to adore.
All the while
I wilted inside.
No longer blooming,
you tossed me away.
Freeing me to ride the wind,
of our storm.
I sank deeper
into the muddied earth,
forgotten.
Nourishing myself with pain's rain,
I rooted I grew,
with only myself.
Sturdy I rose
towards the moon.
For you saw a flower
when I was a tree.

Turmoil

This feeling,
I know it all too well.
Creeps
deep within, begging
to be released.
This surge
of unwelcomed turmoil claws
until my mind is consumed by only it.
I attempt to escape, weary
of the destruction, weary
of the lack of time. I can't run.
I can't neglect this
ticking time bomb.
Ticking ticking
alongside the fall of the sweat,
dripping from my brow.
I can't keep doing this.
I mustn't keep doing, this.
Damn it.

Ponder

Day end,
the sun settled
hours ago,
to allow the stars and moon,
their time to play.
Tired, I lay and ponder,
our journey thus far.
I deflect my tendency to reject
the happiness and contentment
that warms
my heart, even in
a cold bed.
Scenarios, one after another,
bring hope, paired with a smile.
Though only granted
this moment,
this now,
I can't help
but to envision, you and I,
and all the times,
I'll play you'll laugh we'll smile
and experience, your touch
my embrace our intimacy and grow,
with patience
with acceptance
with effort, in love.
And rather,
the story we write ends up
in the history or
current event section,
I know this heart,
tangled with yours,
will never read as fiction.

Your Way

Lifetimes stretched, across
merely decades.
Reason eludes
drawing resentment,
blaming
the blameless.
Taken away,
I searched to replace,
to fill.
Defeated
I raged to all,
to the unknown.
Demanding the way,
with entitlement to answers,
to solutions.
Releasing my sorrow,
my will,
I plead, I cry,
show me the way.
Show me your way.
Looking down in surrender,
peace consumes
at the reflection,
of me
in my creation,
in my pool
of tears.

Truth

Lingering in sorrow
mourning this ideal,
a deepening shadow
concealing ways to heal.
Love's masquerade
tears it apart,
lead astray
by one's own heart.
Intoxicated sight
distorting belief,
the touch you feed
to reality's thief.
Release the truth
to free your soul,
for only you
can make you whole.

Hope

Grateful.
For every fiber in the
fabric of my despair
blankets my heart,
keeping it warm, thawed.
Do not fret at the sadness
behind my eyes, in my voice.
With it I read my lyrics
and sing my song, of hope.
Mourn not.
My innocence merely
feigned, awaits,
eagerly anticipating my return.

Exhale

Starlit sky. Cold.
Visible exhale.
Mind focused on discomfort.
Winter's embrace kissing skin,
bone, and soul.
A rush, unstable footing
gifting fear.
Looking
to the heavens with gratitude.
Knowledge of my discomforts,
my visible exhale,
solidifies reality.
I am alive.

Dare

Blank stare,
yet emotionally content.
Attentive to nothing yet observant to all.
Bewilderment
at the cost of sanity.
Laughter,
a measurement long diluted.
Love, a commodity of little worth.
Dare to dream, dare to embrace.
Don't dare to be caught.
Abnormalities,
best to take the placebo.
Branch away, sink the fangs.
Voids do not require filling.
Place the bet not on kindness,
lean on the scales, balance is fictional.
Speed up the sand, with pleasantries.
Dare to smile, dare to live.
Don't dare to be caught.
Catch me, if you can.

War

Too swift
they assaulted.
As if a volley of arrows
eclipsed my will,
pierced my mind.
Each removal bloodied,
exposing deeper.
Breathing labored,
combating desire to lay down,
to give in, to give up.
The ground, painted
of splinter, tip and flesh.
Yet I stand in my grave,
where I once lay.

Aftermath

As the downpour
quenches the earth,
its shadow,
ominous and powerful,
paves way to rebirth.
The path rising in altitude,
Its peak opening and forcing,
ocular and cerebral enchantment.
A present of the sky.
Its omnipotence,
dominating and tranquil,
painting a picture
hung only in a memory.

Exhume

This necessity,
excruciating and protracted,
will exhume myself.
Hands raw bruised bloody
and aching,
digging through root rubble
and bone.
The unearthing,
a stone sarcophagus tightly sealed,
by apprehension, consternation.
The realization, no tools machinery
or apparatus.
Only flesh, muscle bone
and force of will.
Blood mixing with sweat,
air fleeting my lungs, to pay the toll.

Purpose

Mind wandering effortlessly,
everything and nothing.
Enigmatic history, eluding purpose.
Escaping myself.
No. Come back.
Back to the present, this now,
inside the dark.
Embrace it.
Feel it. Beat it.
Where it lingers is where it dies.
Inside my mind, slain by my heart.

Demands

She demands my essence.
Raw, unfiltered.
Purified
by only the means
of vigilant truth.
Deceived not by ideology,
of environmental conditioning.
Falsities of misplaced desire,
hasty lust.
Every glance,
as if experiencing
the first.
Every touch,
delicate.
She demands
nothing of the world,
that produces
our adulterated realities.
She demands everything
of what our souls, will tie to be.
She demands me,
given in such a way that exists,
only because she demands it.

Candle

My candle provides sight in the dark,
warmth in the cold.
Fighting the elements,
my hand shielding its flame.
A canopy to the rain,
a barrier to the wind.
Much to admire.
The way it dances,
the way it glows
and illuminates
the shadow's graffiti.
Though vigilant
with my hand,
extinguished it still was.
By my own breath
too close in admiration.

Breathe

Racing,
fluttering swiftly
inside my chest,
attempting to keep pace
with my mind.
Breathe,
blanket the chaos
with an embrace of oxygen.
These thoughts are overbearing.
This heart is draining.
Breathe.
It's not enough.
Again.
Breathe.
Find my footing.
Find my earth,
connect and align.
Soul to soul,
bound with ground. Breathe.
Claim the calm.
Breathe.
    Breathe.
        Breathe.

Shame

It is strange,
this phenomenon
of the addict.
Stuck in blame,
repulsed by happiness.

Why?

We all desire it,
so why do we not
gravitate towards it?

What part of us do
we cry into
when the purest
form of joy is our enemy?

Fear or anger?
One in the same.
Fear or sadness?
One in the same.
Shame and guilt.

Inward looking,
I'll place my blame
and snuff my ego,
so I may finally face
the shame and guilt.

Drought

This occurrence,
unexpected drought,
a possibility that eluded
myself and time.
Her embrace like
a soft rain,
nourishing and uplifting the floral.
Her kiss, gentle
like the wind dancing
with the grass,
now pours only in my dreams.
Forever will I wilt until she
eclipses the sun and
bathes me once more.

Awareness

Gentleness of heart, of touch.
Circulating blood
and breath.
Fueling the mind of intellect,
expanding perception and understanding.
Revelations of unity,
of connection,
drawing all together.
Body and mind,
gifted soul.
When three become one,
one becomes all.

Lingering

Though my size blankets
your own, this illusion
reduced me.
To fit not together like
our bodies deceit.
Rather, engulfed
in your palm,
to be released into the bin
as you exit me.
My worth,
a lingering
residue between
your fingers.
There I'll remain.
There we'll die.

Strength

When pride releases
by guilt and shame of sin
beckoned from the soul
into the back of the throat,
forcing itself out
through the lips.
A pure cry of defiance
against the norm.

Help me.

The surrender
from this utterance
combined with honesty,
will lay the foundation for
the evolution needed to survive.

No longer frail.
No longer brittle.
Wielding voice
as the source of growth.

Help me.
What strength
in just two words.

Time Lost

It happened, again.
Time lost
to self-hatred.
Seconds spiraling
between thoughts.
Minutes gifted
to self-destruction.
Days labored
to reach my bottom.
Months
clearing debris
from the path,
of my destruction.
Years lost
to standing
in my own way.
Time lost
to such cruelty never was
time wasted.
For the cost of self-love
was time
spent in hate.

Under It All

Under it I see it,
under it all.
Beneath the chaos,
I see the innocence.
The shine illuminating,
from smile to eyes.
The child yearning, gasping,
for a breath of you.

I see, mixed
between torment
and insanity,
a beauty
awaiting nourishment.

Bloom,
as the magnificent
intoxicating being
under it all.

A Piece

Alluring,
as if a spell created
solely to bewilder the mind,
yet, entrance the heart.
Her beauty,
though compelling,
didn't guide my desire to meld
into her being.
I wanted to exist between
her calming sea of innocence and
her enigmatic inferno of chaos.
In hopes to melt and evaporate,
for her to breathe me in or blow me away.
At least then, I'll know
I became, even if just briefly,
a piece to her
abstract perfection.

Impact

Drawn in by the depth of tales,
written
in our scars.

Caged
by fear.
Shackled
to repetitive wounds.
Released by mutual
vulnerability.

Evacuating logic
so the impact
of our souls
can rewrite our hearts.

Darkness

I started this journey just a little too late.
I haven't reached safety
as the sun sets on my path.
I focus on the beauty of sunset
before it begins. Darkness envelops.
I've been here many times.
This fear, dare not say, unknown,
for the familiarity calms my mind,
slows my breath.
Though nothing illuminates my way,
my step is still guided.
By knowledge gained of success,
of failure and of faith.
Darkness, the fear of the unknown,
has become my ally.
For darkness leads me to me.

Fissure

The air was thick and silent,
similar to our lips, contrary
to our minds.
Though together,
I felt the shift,
quaking before our feet,
as the ground, splitting
like my heart, fissured
like our path, glancing
into the unknown.

I reached unnoticed, hindered by
your glossy eyes,
reflecting nothing more than yourself.
Ground gave way,
oblivious,
you fell
into the void,
of living memories.

Corruption

All things they say come
to an end.
This wasn't something
I could prepare for.
There was no warning no sign,
just eradication.
My lungs fill with
your taste
for the last time.
I'm not ready to live,
to exist without you.
The last drop falls alongside
my heart. Farewell to choice,
to freedom.

Death

Death
does not come with a cloak or scythe.
Nor a horse as dark
as night.
It looks familiar
like me or you.
I've acquired its taste,
its touch
to my desire.
A wish, a plea between lines.
Please,
slow my breathing, eyes heavy,
a gentle sleep into the unknown.
Offering up all that I am,
you've denied me again and again.
A whisper, a chill through bone and soul.
To earn my death,
I must first have a life.

Veil

Who are we
but a reflection of our truth, our deceit.
Venomous babble defecates,
down lip mind
and soul. How much can fill
your cup before choking on your
weaved veil, crafted,
on zeal of truth
you've yet
to embrace.

Still

This,
senseless demeanor stuck on repeat for a
pointless endeavor. Knowing,
I have tools to deal with any
untimely fools, yet
I sit and stir as my line begins
to blur. Conclusion in your will, if only I
could be still.

Surprise

This pleasantry, though overcast with gloom,
ignites and bursts the dreary grays into vibrant
warm colors.
A surprise, simple,
yet heartwarming.
Moments like this remind me,
regardless of the weather,
I can still find a light.

Dozens

Though you started to grow,
to change, to heal
and shatter your chains, to learn,
to feel, to bloom,
and my, how you did.
You feel stuck, lost.
That war I see you wage in the depths
of your amber reflection, with every glance
at every mirror.
Let it go.
The weight you've diminished yet still harbor in your pocket.
The mending of one link doesn't negate
the dozens you've broke.
Though not today, nor yesterday
or even tomorrow,
will the last link sever.
But it will, oh, it will.
If you just keep going.

Contradiction

Skies darken, clouds engulf,
a haze of mind of soul.
Thoughts gust, burst
and funnel in hopes to
batter my will.
On cue,
the downpour of doubt,
tides of despair, entails.
Wave after wave,
weight unbearable
breath unattainable drowning,
inevitable.

Of Storms

Surrendering to fate,
this fury of storms.
Wave
after wave,
carries me to shore.
Lungs heave,
rebirth in each breath.
The same waves that claimed my life,
carried me to my feet.
The same wind lifted,
cradling my weight.
With each step the clouds parted.
A new day guiding my path.
Hope sprouts
and blooms,
fed by the rain.
I thought this storm
wanted my life.
All it intended, its purpose,
was to guide me
to the light.

If I Could

If I could,
I would show you
how the stars dance
in your gaze
as it incites mine to hold
for all of time.
I would show you how
the sparks play
with your touch
as it invokes senses
to your command.
I would show you
how much peace,
effortlessly,
you bring to
my weary mind, tired soul.
I would show you all that
you are within me,
if only I could.

Surrender

Pulsating
faster and louder,
echoed against the walls.
Painted by the rhythm of pain, of blood, top to bottom.
Efforts smear and blend.
Fruitless attempt to cleanse.
Powerless my fury, my rage. Collapsing,
skin to ground. Freedom,
only in defeat.

Mended

Snow,
softly landing to the ground, on my skin.
Igniting wonder and, happiness.
A moment
of darkness, despair
mended sweetly, lovingly,
by mother's kiss.
Gratitude
to feel pain,
to feel sadness.
Amplifying and enriching, a world's gift
of awe
and joy.

Whisper

My lips struggle to piece together the words to break our silence.

Our eyes align into longing that overpowers our voice.

Hearts aching to dance
in the warmth of our embrace.

Thoughts pacing back and forth, restraining desire of tattered souls.

All that we are, lost before
our beginning, due to one,

neglected whisper.

Duet

What will it take to let you go?
You're the one still holding on.
I just want to live in peace.
Why is there blood on your hands then?
I can live this life on my own.
How?
I can find balance without you.
Wouldn't that be easier with all of you?
How would you know, being gone so long...
You're a fool if you think I ever left.
Then where are you?
Where you left me.
I've dug everywhere looking for you.
You won't find me with dirt on your hands.
Enough, I deserve to be happy.
Are you sure you're ready for that?
I am.
Then let go.
Of what?
You.

Ocean

Wave after wave
endlessly building to climax,
roaring and crashing, spreading out
over and through,
consuming every inch along the way.
Significant beauty.
Efficient destruction.
Lyrics reaching the heart,
song entrancing the mind.
Taken in deeply to the core,
openly embracing the fury within.
Looking to embrace the now,
the present,
feeling the breeze absorb,
turning to the ocean
to calm the one,
inside my mind.

Say It

Reluctantly,
I keep my solicitude shrouded,
gently concealed
by obsessive tendencies.
Teetering between hope and fear,
awaiting the right moment
or outright abolishment.
Thoughts oscillate,
between contentment and yearning,
as if pulsating alongside my beating heart.
Say it, say it…say it.
I shouldn't.
Self-loathing dancing
in rhythm with self-worth,
captivating an audience
of desire and affection.
Desire swaying on what ifs.
Affection standing firm,
on what is.
Fickleness between
gullible emotion and pure logic
enabling unjust heartache and despair.
This raging contradiction of heart and mind,
impetuous attrition,
weighs heavily on the soul.
Say it, say it…say it!
I won't.

Tether

Moonlight draws my curious eyes,
dancing among clouds in which it lies.
My lungs fill with crisp night air,
the breeze gently grazes my skin left bare.
The trees and wildlife sing a loving tune,
my heart providing the beat for my mind to swoon.
Gifted by nature, this invigorating moment
allowing temporary release from artificial torment.
Mother desperately calling to break my tether,
freeing my soul for us
to finally be together.

Desire

Qualities I have missed
have started to ignite.
A flame of passion,
engulfing my being.
Desire once known
begins to flood my mind.
Filtering and cleansing
the filth of decay,
A steady pulse carries
the want to live,
and love.
I wonder how long
this fantasy will linger.
My fear intrudes
swiftly to blanket the flame.
Lungs desperately fighting
to fan the fleeting embers.
Hands grasping,
for anything,
as weight shifts to ash.
My desire
starts with hope
yet ends with despair.
Terrified to reach further
for what I want.

Mold

I watched as you did nothing.
The embodiment of strength
and protection crippled
my belief of a father,
while simultaneously creating
the mold of my future.
The cries fell on your ears silently,
though deaf you are not.
The hands reaching for yours
fell limply into a pit of despair,
though crippled, you are not.
Though you cast my mold,
your soul will quake to
the sound of my hammer,
forging the shield
 that I will lift alongside
the mantle of protector
that you failed to wear.

Treasure

I can take a trip to any place
any time within my life,
simply by navigating
my map written and drawn
by my scars.
Though its creation
took the hands of myself
and of many others, only I
can read it.

It took some time to realize
it was a map to amazing treasure.
So, I grabbed a shovel
and started my journey.
I stopped at every scar.

I dug.

Some were deep
some were shallow
but all were worth my effort.
I collected my treasure
from every hole, every scar,
knowing time would fill them properly.
I laid my findings on my table,
with relief I smiled,
as the treasure was
nothing more than
the finding of me.

I am

This notion as if
I'm meant to understand,
is uniquely human and purely ego.
I am no more, no less than
the grass I lay on.
I am the roots burrowing
in the depths of earth.
My heart beats
just as evenly as the
rhythm of the birds' song.
I am just as beautiful
as the fog blanketing
the morning
view of towering mountains.
I am the rivers that bend,
the sea that waves,
the stars that burn,
eventually to return to nothing,
while remaining all.
I am the past
as much as future existing
only in now.
I am you,
just as you…
are me.
And only when we align
like an eclipse of souls
in humility, will we see
our place is not to question,
rather to just be.

Perspective

I watched as the color
drained from my world,
as if I had accidentally
spilled paint thinner on
my canvas.
I had spent years painting.
The sorrow and despair
blended as swiftly
as the melting colors.
Frantically, I struggled
to stop the spread,
my desperation only
amplified the chaos.
In defeat, my frustration,
I threw my canvas, my world.
As I walked away,
I looked back and
stopped dead in my tracks.
My world
once again filled with color
as I saw my efforts,
my canvas
was just as beautiful.
I only needed
to step back to see,
a new perspective.

Voiceless

I'm sorry,
this isn't how I meant to live.
I know you're upset,
I've said it until my face,
turned blue, breathless,
know now my words
were always true.
I'm so sorry, mother
and father,
I never wanted
you to bury your son
or daughter.
I never knew
my inability to cope
would lead to dope,
or tie the rope that hung
from the rafter, writing
my final chapter.
I'm so sorry,
to my son or daughter,
you'll have to live, without
a mother or father.
I never meant, to leave you all alone,
it's a sin I won't be able to atone.
I begged to God for my release,
I'm so sorry only in
my coffin did I finally
find my peace.

Proud

I was good, I swear it.
I got the grades I studied hard,
to make you proud, mother.
I was kind and gentle
wouldn't hurt a fly,
aren't you proud, Mother?
I grew strong and smart
and began to question.
Wasn't I enough to make you proud, Mother?
I rebelled to your control,
to your belittlement and abuse.
I stood up for myself.
You should be proud, Mother.
I failed to learn how to cope
with pain, but pushed on day after day
till I learned how.
Your son is an addict,
 a father, a worker, a lover
and a fighter, but always
a gentleman
who offers his hand to those,
on the ground.
You would be proud, mother.
I found a home and a family
who loves me for me.
A daughter that's proud
to call me father.
But you know,
in this gorgeous life of mine,
what I'm most proud of
is the fact,
that I no longer care if you are proud.

View From Above

As a trucker, we see it all.
We see you singing along, even dancing
to your favorite song.
We watch as you fight
with your passenger to your right.
We wave back to your kids
and laugh at open gas lids.
We see it all,
from Mini Coopers
to big black Escalades, and yes,
even your naughty escapades.
Mile after mile,
we smile and laugh,
normally at your behalf.
We watch as you drive distracted
into the rear
of the car you've compacted.
From texts and tweets,
your head is bobbing,
or alcohol and drugs,
your head is nodding,
that child is mangled,
a mother now sobbing.
We see it all,
from good to bad to funny and mad.
Despite it all, I'm still in love,
with the view from above.

Meant To Be

I have to shift,
I have to change,
even if it hurts
or feels too strange.
I'll share my pain
and raise my voice,
strongly declaring
I've made this choice.
I know the problem
lies within me,
it took so much to finally see.
I'll start right away
with belief and attitude,
opening my mind
to unforeseen magnitude.
I'll own it all,
accepting my own fault
to bring my fear
and anger to a halt.
I won't hide any longer
from shame or guilt,
I'll tear down the frame
of the bed I built.
With help from others
and brand-new lumber,
I'll build a new one for me to slumber.
I'll give up my time to those in need,
making new bonds
for my soul to feed.
I'll learn and grow into the best of me,
closing my eyes,
knowing all is as it's meant to be.

It Was Just

It was just a line of blow,
how was I supposed to know?
It was just a joint
from a friend,
we didn't know
all the fun would end.
It was just a pill an opioid,
I only intended to fill a void.
It was just a party,
having a blast, for most of us,
it would be our last.
It was just enough,
barely traced,
No one knew, these all
had been laced.
It was just a drug,
called Fentanyl.
We didn't know,
it would take it all.

Addiction

Pain sundered my soul,
leaving a corpse
with a beating heart.
My blood still warm,
I had never been so cold.
I hurt,
so I hurt others.
I lied and manipulated,
till you fed
from my tainted palm,
while I fed my chaos,
my addiction that I disguised as comfort.
I fed until my sundered soul,
swelled and ruptured, becoming shrapnel
to remove once resurfaced.
Twenty years later,
I finally collected all the pieces.
I sat down to put it back together.
I became overwhelmed,
I didn't know what I was doing.
I heard a laugh,
as they approached me.
"We've worked this puzzle before,
would you like some help?"
In desperation, I said yes,
and they taught me.
"These pieces are shame,
throw them away."
"These pieces are guilt,
throw them away."
"These pieces are honesty,
they belong in the center."
"These are love and hope,
they surround honesty."

As we placed the last piece,
I feared it wouldn't hold.
"For the final step,
to hold it all together...
Just make it through today
and teach the next person,
struggling with their pieces."

Her Sea

She draws me in,
beginning with her eyes.
The draw of her radiant blue
ushers exploration
of the depth of her sea.
Her soul, the lighthouse
that guides me to safety, and
shelters my heart
from weather, from harm.
I map her body with curiosity
and desire.
Noting her scars,
like a battle-worn Goddess,
claiming my body as her
prize. Our embrace pulls,
like the gravity of the sun, as
it heats our hearts,
our bodies as she melts
around me and I,
releasing my love as her sea,
her depths
quake around me.

Garden

We walked,
through the garden
we created.
though I looked behind
a little too late.
I panicked.
Wilt and Decay,
followed your every step.
I turned to you,
in disbelief
as your ground crumbled.
My heart sank, along with you
into your bottom.
Even though I know
the way out,
I couldn't jump in.
I searched for anything
to pull you out.
I ripped open my chest
and fashioned a rope,
from every vein anchored by my heart.
It wasn't enough.
I couldn't pull your weight
and nearly fell in.
Clinging to the edge bleeding out,
I stitched my wounds, with the roots
of our garden.
As I walked away,
defeated and hopeless I watched as
my own steps began to wilt and decay.
As my ground gave way,
I laughed all the way down.
For I know the way out.

Graffiti

I reached
for the sky in hopes
to dance with the clouds.
I reached in hopes
to echo my song
alongside the boom
of thunder.
I reached in hopes
to illuminate the world
like lightning.
I reached for the sky
knowing I am
afraid of heights.
I reached the
peak of my ascension,
feeling peace
for only a moment before
the fall.
Even still I'll
reach to leave my mark,
even if it is only as graffiti,
on the ground.

Fire

I never knew
how well the flames
would dance
in my hands
or the comfort it
would offer against the ice
encasing my heart.
And my god do they dance
even more so in my eyes,
leaving you to wonder
if the intensity is passion
or rage.
But as my comfort
in the fire grew,
I gifted it
with every touch
and every glance.
And as my fury
of passionate rage engulfed
all that I love,
it eventually turned
even on me,
incinerating myself
leaving only ash
and the sound
of sizzling tears.
Fortunately,
like a phoenix
I rose from my ashes
and learned
to play with
water instead.

Mirror

I can walk
through the forest
in the blackness of night,
or the cemetery in search
of the restless,
or place me in a room
with criminals and addicts,
or stand me
at the head of a crowd
and tell me to speak
and I can do
all of these at most
just a little bit nervous.
But if the goal
is to get me
to show fear,
simply ask me
to look in a mirror.

Mystery

And though our tangled hearts
never read as fiction
like all books,
the story came to an end
leaving us
wanting.
Just another sentence
another paragraph
another page,
a chapter a sequel.
Just a taste
of the ink
that made my heart soar
on the blank pages
of our unknown.
I'll place it
back on the shelf
in the history section.
And pick a new one from mystery.

Not a Poem

I expect it won't be swift, or merciful. I'll be off camping somewhere in the northwest, just taking in the beauty of nature in the mountains. It'll happen in broad daylight, so I see it coming. I'll run, in vain, to escape my long overdue fate. They'll chase, slowly, teasing hope of escaping the inevitable. Heart racing, lungs frantically struggling to fill. The attrition on my adrenaline-fueled muscles will finally bring me to my knees. I'll pull and drag my quivering body against a tree, facing death as it draws near.

Slowly they creep around me, the sleuth of bears. Their breath is warm, so close, it is almost comforting. How naïve to think I'd get away with selfishly indulging for so long. Teeth bearing, I reach in my bag for the very reason for their vengeful wrath. They let out a frightening bellow as I take my last bite...of a bear claw.

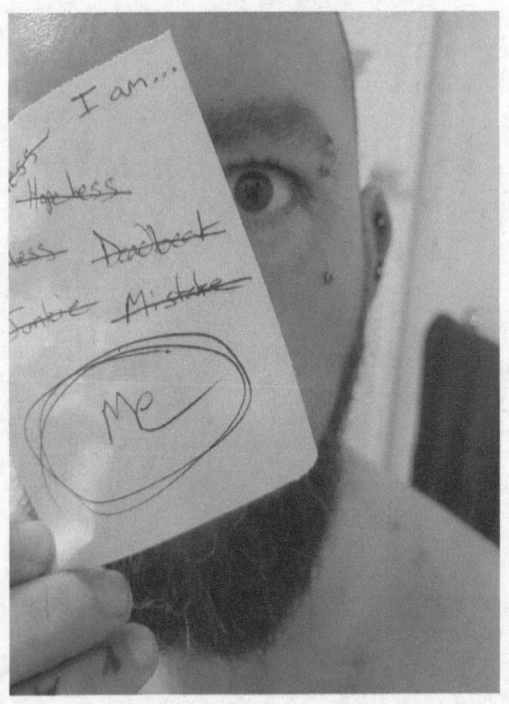

Cory Beasley is northern-born and southern-raised. A hard-working man that's finally stepped into the light after living in the dark for decades. On a mission to help others find the positive in an all too negative world.

"I TRY MY BEST TO LIVE A LIFE OF HONESTY AND CARRY A MESSAGE OF HOPE. WHO I AM IS AN IMPOSSIBLE THING TO RELAY, FOR I AM ALWAYS LEARNING AND GROWING INTO SOMETHING MORE."

Find more from Cory: